Adult MAD LIBS

The world's greatest _drinking_ game

BYO Mad Libs

by Jay Perrone

PSS!
PRICE STERN SLOAN
An Imprint of Penguin Group (USA) Inc.

PRICE STERN SLOAN
Published by the Penguin Group
Penguin Group (USA) Inc., 375 Hudson Street, New York, New York 10014, USA
Penguin Group (Canada), 90 Eglinton Avenue East, Suite 700, Toronto, Ontario M4P 2Y3, Canada
(a division of Pearson Penguin Canada Inc.)
Penguin Books Ltd, 80 Strand, London WC2R 0RL, England
Penguin Ireland, 25 St Stephen's Green, Dublin 2, Ireland (a division of Penguin Books Ltd)
Penguin Group (Australia), 707 Collins Street, Melbourne, Victoria 3008, Australia
(a division of Pearson Australia Group Pty Ltd)
Penguin Books India Pvt Ltd, 11 Community Centre, Panchsheel Park, New Delhi—110 017, India
Penguin Group (NZ), 67 Apollo Drive, Rosedale, Auckland 0632, New Zealand (a division of Pearson New Zealand Ltd)
Penguin Books (South Africa), Rosebank Office Park, 181 Jan Smuts Avenue, Parktown North 2193, South Africa
Penguin China, B7 Jiaming Center, 27 East Third Ring Road North, Chaoyang District, Beijing 100020, China

Penguin Books Ltd, Registered Offices: 80 Strand, London WC2R 0RL, England

Published by Price Stern Sloan,
a division of Penguin Young Readers Group,
345 Hudson Street, New York, New York 10014.

ISBN 978-0-8431-7294-2
1 3 5 7 9 10 8 6 4 2

ALWAYS LEARNING   **PEARSON**

MAD LIBS® is a game for people who don't like games! It can be played by one, two, three, four, or forty.

• RIDICULOUSLY SIMPLE DIRECTIONS

In this book, you'll find stories containing blank spaces where words are left out. One player, the READER, selects one of the stories. The READER shouldn't tell anyone what the story is about. Instead, the READER should ask the other players, the WRITERS, to give words to fill in the blank spaces in the story.

• TO PLAY

The READER asks each WRITER in turn to call out words—adjectives or nouns or whatever the spaces call for—and uses them to fill in the blank spaces in the story. The result is your very own MAD LIBS! Then, when the READER reads the completed MAD LIBS to the other players, they will discover they have written a story that is fantastic, screamingly funny, shocking, silly, crazy, or just plain dumb—depending on the words each WRITER called out.

• EXAMPLE (*Before* and *After*)

" _____ !" he said _____
  EXCLAMATION   ADVERB

as he jumped into his convertible _____ and
                                                    NOUN

drove off with his _____ wife.
                          ADJECTIVE

" ___*Ouch*___ !" he said ___*stupidly*___
  EXCLAMATION   ADVERB

as he jumped into his convertible ___*cat*___ and
                                                    NOUN

drove off with his ___*brave*___ wife.
                          ADJECTIVE

In case you have forgotten what adjectives, adverbs, nouns, and verbs are, here is a quick review:

An **ADJECTIVE** describes something or somebody. *Lumpy*, *soft*, *ugly*, *messy*, and *short* are adjectives.

An **ADVERB** tells how something is done. It modifies a verb and usually ends in "ly." *Modestly*, *stupidly*, *greedily*, and *carefully* are adverbs.

A **NOUN** is the name of a person, place, or thing. *Sidewalk*, *umbrella*, *bridle*, *bathtub*, and *nose* are nouns.

A **VERB** is an action word. *Run*, *pitch*, *jump*, and *swim* are verbs. Put the verbs in past tense if the directions say **PAST TENSE**. *Ran*, *pitched*, *jumped*, and *swam* are verbs in the past tense.

When we ask for **A PLACE**, we mean any sort of place: a country or city (*Spain*, *Cleveland*) or a room (*bathroom*, *kitchen*).

An **EXCLAMATION** or **SILLY WORD** is any sort of funny sound, gasp, grunt, or outcry, like *Wow!*, *Ouch!*, *Whomp!*, *Ick!*, and *Gadzooks!*

When we ask for specific words, like a **NUMBER**, a **COLOR**, an **ANIMAL**, or a **PART OF THE BODY**, we mean a word that is one of those things, like *seven*, *blue*, *horse*, or *head*.

When we ask for a **PLURAL**, it means more than one. For example, *cat* pluralized is *cats*.

Adult
MAD LIBS
THE LAST TEST TILL FREEDOM
The world's greatest *drinking* game

MAD LIBS® is fun to play with friends, but you can also play it by yourself! To begin with, DO NOT look at the story on the page below. Fill in the blanks on this page with the words called for. Then, using the words you have selected, fill in the blank spaces in the story. Now you've created your own hilarious MAD LIBS® game!

EXCLAMATION _____

NOUN _____

VERB _____

NUMBER _____

NOUN _____

NOUN _____

VERB (PAST TENSE) _____

NOUN _____

PLURAL NOUN _____

ADJECTIVE _____

COLOR _____

PERSON IN ROOM _____

NUMBER _____

NOUN _____

ADJECTIVE _____

PLURAL NOUN _____

ADJECTIVE _____

EXCLAMATION _____

THE LAST TEST TILL FREEDOM

_____ —it's the _____ I've been waiting for all year:
 EXCLAMATION   NOUN

the final test before summer vacation! But how am I supposed to

_____ on this exam when summer is just _____
 VERB   NUMBER

minutes away?! I look at my blank _____ booklet sitting
                                        NOUN

next to my graphing _____ . Maybe I should have
                          NOUN

_____ more for this test. After all, _____ is not
 VERB (PAST TENSE)   NOUN

my best subject. I answer the first few _____ on the test,
                                              PLURAL NOUN

and I'm starting to feel _____ when I see that my
                              ADJECTIVE

_____ -noser classmate _____ is _____
 COLOR   PERSON IN ROOM   NUMBER

sections ahead. I decide to put the _____ to the metal and
                                          NOUN

really concentrate on answering these _____ questions.
                                            ADJECTIVE

"Please put down your _____ . Time is up," the teacher
                            PLURAL NOUN

announces. I fill in the _____ bubble with my pencil just as
                              ADJECTIVE

time expires. _____ ! It's finally time for summer!
                EXCLAMATION

MAD LIBS® is fun to play with friends, but you can also play it by yourself! To begin with, DO NOT look at the story on the page below. Fill in the blanks on this page with the words called for. Then, using the words you have selected, fill in the blank spaces in the story. Now you've created your own hilarious MAD LIBS® game!

ADJECTIVE _____

PERSON IN ROOM (FEMALE) _____

ADJECTIVE _____

VERB ENDING IN "ING" _____

EXCLAMATION _____

ADJECTIVE _____

PART OF THE BODY _____

ADVERB _____

PART OF THE BODY (PLURAL) _____

VERB _____

ADJECTIVE _____

TYPE OF LIQUID _____

NUMBER _____

VERB ENDING IN "ING" _____

SAME PERSON IN ROOM (FEMALE) _____

NOUN _____

ADVERB _____

NOUN _____

ALMOST STICKING THE LANDING

The public pool is my favorite place to be during the summer. It gets

so _____ in my apartment, the pool is the only place to find
　　　　　ADJECTIVE

any relief. It is also one of the few places I get to see _____ ,
　　　　　　　　　　　　　　　　　　　　　　　　　　　　　　PERSON IN ROOM (FEMALE)

the _____ lifeguard. Now . . . how to get her attention? I
　　　　ADJECTIVE

decide to jump off the _____ board. " _____!" I
　　　　　　　　　　　　VERB ENDING IN "ING"　　　　EXCLAMATION

think to myself as I begin my _____ climb to the top.
　　　　　　　　　　　　　　　　　　ADJECTIVE

My _____ beats _____ and sweat drips from
　　PART OF THE BODY　　　　ADVERB

my _____ . Finally, I reach the top and slowly _____
　　PART OF THE BODY (PLURAL)　　　　　　　　　　　　　　　　　　VERB

to the edge. I take a/an _____ breath and jump into the
　　　　　　　　　　　　ADJECTIVE

_____ . After what seems like _____ hours, I swim
TYPE OF LIQUID　　　　　　　　　　　　NUMBER

to the surface only to hear everyone _____ at me, including
　　　　　　　　　　　　　　　　　　VERB ENDING IN "ING"

_____ . It's only then that I realize—my _____
SAME PERSON IN ROOM (FEMALE)　　　　　　　　　　　　　　　　NOUN

came completely off and I am _____ naked! Looks like I'll
　　　　　　　　　　　　　　ADVERB

be using the _____ conditioner at home to stay cool from
　　　　　　　NOUN

now on!

Adult MAD LIBS

The world's greatest *drinking* game

HOW TO DEAL WITH SUMMER SNOBBERY

MAD LIBS® is fun to play with friends, but you can also play it by yourself! To begin with, DO NOT look at the story on the page below. Fill in the blanks on this page with the words called for. Then, using the words you have selected, fill in the blank spaces in the story. Now you've created your own hilarious MAD LIBS® game!

VERB _____

ADJECTIVE _____

CELEBRITY _____

ADJECTIVE _____

A PLACE _____

VERB _____

PLURAL NOUN _____

PLURAL NOUN _____

PART OF THE BODY _____

A PLACE _____

ADJECTIVE _____

NOUN _____

PLURAL NOUN _____

ADVERB _____

NUMBER _____

VERB (PAST TENSE) _____

VERB _____

PART OF THE BODY _____

Let's face it: Rich people can _____ . Most of us have at least

VERB

one _____ friend who has more money than _____

ADJECTIVE — CELEBRITY

and loves to brag about it. Even worse is when they talk about all the

_____ places they go for the summer while you're stuck at

ADJECTIVE

(the) _____ wanting to _____ yourself. Fortunately,

A PLACE — VERB

there is a three-step solution to help you deal with these insufferable

_____ :

PLURAL NOUN

1. When forced to talk with rich _____ about vacations,

PLURAL NOUN

   always lie your _____ off. If your rich friend is going to

PART OF THE BODY

   (the) _____ , say you are going, too!

A PLACE

2. Your _____ friends will have to tell you about how

ADJECTIVE

   they're getting to their destination, whether it's by plane

   or by _____ . Have some fun with the situation by

NOUN

   saying, "You know, _____ have been known to

PLURAL NOUN

   _____ combust. _____ people _____ last

ADVERB — NUMBER — VERB (PAST TENSE)

   year using them!"

3. If all else fails, simply _____ them in the _____ .

VERB — PART OF THE BODY

MAD LIBS® is fun to play with friends, but you can also play it by yourself! To begin with, DO NOT look at the story on the page below. Fill in the blanks on this page with the words called for. Then, using the words you have selected, fill in the blank spaces in the story. Now you've created your own hilarious MAD LIBS® game!

PERSON IN ROOM (FEMALE) _____

ADJECTIVE _____

COLOR _____

ADJECTIVE _____

VERB _____

ADJECTIVE _____

NOUN _____

VERB _____

ADJECTIVE _____

VERB ENDING IN "ING" _____

PART OF THE BODY _____

VERB _____

PART OF THE BODY _____

PART OF THE BODY (PLURAL) _____

PLURAL NOUN _____

ADJECTIVE _____

NUMBER _____

NOUN _____

Adult MAD LIBS™ SUMMER LOVIN'

The world's greatest _drinking_ game

You are at the beach and _____ is there. She is looking super

PERSON IN ROOM (FEMALE)

_____ in that _____ bikini. You have had such a/

ADJECTIVE   COLOR

an _____ crush on her and all you want is to _____

ADJECTIVE   VERB

her out on a date. Here's some _____ advice to help seal the

ADJECTIVE

_____:

NOUN

- _____ the ice. Casually start a conversation about

VERB

  the _____ weather you've had lately or where her

ADJECTIVE

  family is _____ for vacation. Keep it simple!

VERB ENDING IN "ING"

- Pay attention to her body language. Is she playing with her

  _____? Does she _____ at your jokes? Does

PART OF THE BODY   VERB

  she bite her lower _____ when you compliment her?

PART OF THE BODY

- When she's talking, look directly into her _____.

PART OF THE BODY (PLURAL)

  Girls always notice when you're looking at their _____!

PLURAL NOUN

- Ask for her number. If she's _____, she'll give it to

ADJECTIVE

  you. Just make sure to call her the next day and not

  _____ days later. She'll think you're a/an _____!

NUMBER   NOUN

MAD LIBS® is fun to play with friends, but you can also play it by yourself! To begin with, DO NOT look at the story on the page below. Fill in the blanks on this page with the words called for. Then, using the words you have selected, fill in the blank spaces in the story. Now you've created your own hilarious MAD LIBS® game!

ADJECTIVE _____

NOUN _____

NOUN _____

ADJECTIVE _____

ADJECTIVE _____

VERB _____

ADJECTIVE _____

PLURAL NOUN _____

VERB ENDING IN "ING" _____

EXCLAMATION _____

PERSON IN ROOM (MALE) _____

VERB _____

ADVERB _____

VERB _____

NOUN _____

ADJECTIVE _____

VERB ENDING IN "ING" _____

NOUN _____

Ah, another year at Camp _____ _____ . You
ADJECTIVE NOUN

spent many summers here as a camper and have decided to delay

adulthood by coming back to work as a/an _____ . It's a/an
NOUN

_____ gig: decent pay, lots of _____ coworkers to
ADJECTIVE ADJECTIVE

_____ with around the campfire, and plenty of time spent
VERB

in the _____ outdoors. On your first day, you drop your
ADJECTIVE

group of ten-year-olds off at _____ and Crafts. Afterward,
PLURAL NOUN

you put them in two lines to take them _____ in the pool.
VERB ENDING IN "ING"

But when you count the troop, you realize you have a big problem:

One is missing! _____! "Where's _____?" you ask
EXCLAMATION PERSON IN ROOM (MALE)

the rest of the group. All of them _____ their shoulders. You
VERB

_____ run around to find him: You _____ in the
ADVERB VERB

cabins, in the _____, even the _____ tree near the
NOUN ADJECTIVE

lake. Just when all hope seems lost, you hear _____ coming
VERB ENDING IN "ING"

from the bathroom. The little _____ was hiding there the
NOUN

whole time!

From ADULT MAD LIBS™: BYO Mad Libs • Copyright © 2013 by Price Stern Sloan, an imprint of Penguin Group (USA) Inc., 345 Hudson Street, New York, NY 10014.

Adult MAD LIBS ACT YOUR AGE

The world's greatest *drinking* game

MAD LIBS® is fun to play with friends, but you can also play it by yourself! To begin with, DO NOT look at the story on the page below. Fill in the blanks on this page with the words called for. Then, using the words you have selected, fill in the blank spaces in the story. Now you've created your own hilarious MAD LIBS® game!

SILLY WORD _____

NOUN _____

PLURAL NOUN _____

TYPE OF LIQUID _____

PERSON IN ROOM _____

NUMBER _____

NUMBER _____

NOUN _____

COLOR _____

CELEBRITY _____

PART OF THE BODY _____

TYPE OF LIQUID _____

ADVERB _____

NOUN _____

ADJECTIVE _____

PART OF THE BODY _____

PART OF THE BODY (PLURAL) _____

NUMBER _____

NOUN _____

NUMBER _____

_____! I'm so excited to go to my first real _____

SILLY WORD   NOUN

party complete with _____ to hook up with and

PLURAL NOUN

_____ to drink. Only problem? The host, _____,

TYPE OF LIQUID   PERSON IN ROOM

asked me to bring a/an _____-pack of beer . . . and I'm

NUMBER

not _____ years old yet! Good thing I have an ID. But

NUMBER

even though my ID is real, the _____ looks nothing like

NOUN

me! For starters, the guy has _____ hair while mine is

COLOR

brown. He also has a tattoo on his face like _____. But I

CELEBRITY

can't show up empty-_____-ed. I grab the _____

PART OF THE BODY   TYPE OF LIQUID

and _____ walk to the checkout counter. "ID please?"

ADVERB

I casually hand the _____ behind the counter my ID,

NOUN

trying to look _____. I can feel my _____ racing

ADJECTIVE   PART OF THE BODY

and my _____ starting to sweat. After what seems like

PART OF THE BODY (PLURAL)

_____ hours, he asks, "_____ or credit card?" I hand

NUMBER   NOUN

him the cash and walk out. I can't wait to actually be _____

NUMBER

years old.

From ADULT MAD LIBS™: BYO Mad Libs • Copyright © 2013 by Price Stern Sloan, an imprint of Penguin Group (USA) Inc., 345 Hudson Street, New York, NY 10014.

THE GRILL MASTER

The world's greatest *drinking* game

MAD LIBS® is fun to play with friends, but you can also play it by yourself! To begin with, DO NOT look at the story on the page below. Fill in the blanks on this page with the words called for. Then, using the words you have selected, fill in the blank spaces in the story. Now you've created your own hilarious MAD LIBS® game!

VERB ENDING IN "ING" _____

VERB _____

ADJECTIVE _____

LETTER OF THE ALPHABET _____

PLURAL NOUN _____

ADJECTIVE _____

ADJECTIVE _____

VERB (PAST TENSE) _____

VERB _____

ADJECTIVE _____

NOUN _____

ADJECTIVE _____

PERSON IN ROOM _____

ADJECTIVE _____

PART OF THE BODY _____

VERB _____

ANIMAL _____

VERB _____

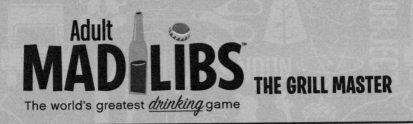
One of the best parts of summer? Your annual block party, of course!

This year, you are in charge of ＿＿＿＿＿＿ all the food. You

VERB ENDING IN "ING"

can ＿＿＿＿＿＿ well, sure, but that is a lot of ＿＿＿＿＿＿

VERB ADJECTIVE

responsibility! Good thing you brought your ＿＿＿＿＿＿ game.

LETTER OF THE ALPHABET

It's the day of the party, and the ＿＿＿＿＿＿ are covered in

PLURAL NOUN

sauce and smell ＿＿＿＿＿＿ . The vegetables are ＿＿＿＿＿＿

ADJECTIVE ADJECTIVE

and ＿＿＿＿＿＿ to perfection. You ＿＿＿＿＿＿ an ice-

VERB (PAST TENSE) VERB

＿＿＿＿＿＿ beer and fire up the ＿＿＿＿＿＿ as guests begin

ADJECTIVE NOUN

to arrive. You throw a few burgers and ＿＿＿＿＿＿ dogs on the

ADJECTIVE

grill. After a few minutes, the first batch is ready. ＿＿＿＿＿＿

PERSON IN ROOM

takes a/an ＿＿＿＿＿＿ bite and pats you on your ＿＿＿＿＿＿

ADJECTIVE PART OF THE BODY

in approval. Your wife comes over to ＿＿＿＿＿＿ you on the cheek.

VERB

It's official—everyone loves your ＿＿＿＿＿＿ burgers! Hey—what

ANIMAL

they don't know won't ＿＿＿＿＿＿ them!

VERB

Adult
MAD LIBS
The world's greatest *drinking* game

DON'T BURN TO A CRISP!

MAD LIBS® is fun to play with friends, but you can also play it by yourself! To begin with, DO NOT look at the story on the page below. Fill in the blanks on this page with the words called for. Then, using the words you have selected, fill in the blank spaces in the story. Now you've created your own hilarious MAD LIBS® game!

EXCLAMATION _____

COLOR _____

ADJECTIVE _____

ARTICLE OF CLOTHING _____

A PLACE _____

VERB _____

NOUN _____

NUMBER _____

VERB _____

NOUN _____

ADJECTIVE _____

VERB _____

COLOR _____

NUMBER _____

VERB _____

PART OF THE BODY _____

ADJECTIVE _____

CELEBRITY _____

_____, your skin is pasty _____! It is such a/an
EXCLAMATION   COLOR

_____ sight that you are embarrassed to take your
ADJECTIVE

_____ off in public. It doesn't help that all your friends
ARTICLE OF CLOTHING

went on that trip to (the) _____ a few weeks ago and have
                          A PLACE

nice, even tans. Next week is the first party of the summer, so you

better get a tan—and fast! After all, you don't want to _____
                                                        VERB

yourself in front of everyone looking white as a/an _____.
                                                    NOUN

You have the day off from work, so why not tan on the back deck

for an hour or _____? You pick a nice lounge chair to
               NUMBER

_____ out on. Next you have to choose the right strength
VERB

of _____-block. This is a/an _____ decision. Too
   NOUN   ADJECTIVE

strong? You will not _____. Too weak? You'll burn and
                     VERB

turn bright _____. SPF _____? Perfect. Now, you
            COLOR   NUMBER

_____ yourself from head to _____ and lie down,
VERB   PART OF THE BODY

making sure it's even so you don't get _____ tan lines. Set an
                                       ADJECTIVE

alarm and relax. In a few hours, you'll look just like _____!
                                                       CELEBRITY

Adult
MAD LIBS

A LESSON IN WATER SPORTS

The world's greatest *drinking* game

MAD LIBS® is fun to play with friends, but you can also play it by yourself! To begin with, DO NOT look at the story on the page below. Fill in the blanks on this page with the words called for. Then, using the words you have selected, fill in the blank spaces in the story. Now you've created your own hilarious MAD LIBS® game!

ADJECTIVE _____

A PLACE _____

ADVERB _____

PART OF THE BODY (PLURAL) _____

PERSON IN ROOM (MALE) _____

NUMBER _____

ADJECTIVE _____

NOUN _____

PART OF THE BODY _____

ADJECTIVE _____

ADJECTIVE _____

TYPE OF LIQUID _____

PLURAL NOUN _____

NUMBER _____

PART OF THE BODY _____

VERB _____

SAME VERB _____

ADJECTIVE _____

A LESSON IN WATER SPORTS

The world's greatest _drinking_ game

Wading in the _____ water on Lake _____ , I
                    ADJECTIVE   A PLACE

_____ grip the water skis between my _____ . My
ADVERB   PART OF THE BODY (PLURAL)

buddy _____ captains the _____ -foot motorboat
       PERSON IN ROOM (MALE)   NUMBER

while my girlfriend shouts instructions to me. I've never gone

water-skiing before. In my _____ dreams, I'll be able to
                            ADJECTIVE

water-ski like a/an _____ and do tricks like standing on one
                     NOUN

_____ while I wave to everyone on the shore. I finally feel
PART OF THE BODY

_____ enough to give it a try, so I wave to my friend to start
ADJECTIVE

the engine. The _____ motor roars to life, and I try to pull
                 ADJECTIVE

myself up out of the _____ . But before I know it, I fall off of
                      TYPE OF LIQUID

my _____ and I'm back in the water. Even though there are
    PLURAL NOUN

_____ gallons of water in my nose, I raise my _____
NUMBER   PART OF THE BODY

to show I'm okay. Almost had it! "Next time," my buddy replies, "let

the boat _____ you, don't _____ the boat." Easy for
          VERB   SAME VERB

him to say. He's driving the _____ thing!
                              ADJECTIVE

MAD LIBS® is fun to play with friends, but you can also play it by yourself! To begin with, DO NOT look at the story on the page below. Fill in the blanks on this page with the words called for. Then, using the words you have selected, fill in the blank spaces in the story. Now you've created your own hilarious MAD LIBS® game!

ADJECTIVE _____

NUMBER _____

VERB _____

NOUN _____

ARTICLE OF CLOTHING (PLURAL) _____

ADJECTIVE _____

ADVERB _____

ADJECTIVE _____

PLURAL NOUN _____

ADJECTIVE _____

PLURAL NOUN _____

ADJECTIVE _____

ADJECTIVE _____

ADJECTIVE _____

VERB _____

NOUN _____

NOUN _____

PART OF THE BODY (PLURAL) _____

INDEPENDENCE DAY

The Fourth of July is the most _____ holiday—even better
ADJECTIVE

than Christmas and Valentine's Day. Why? Here is a list of reasons

why the Fourth of July is # _____ :
NUMBER

- It's a day to _____ America's victory in the
  VERB

  Revolutionary _____ , when we beat the
  NOUN

  _____ off of the British.
  ARTICLE OF CLOTHING (PLURAL)

- The air always smells _____ on the Fourth of July,
  ADJECTIVE

  like a mix of _____-cut grass, _____ barbeque,
  ADVERB   ADJECTIVE

  and burning fire_____!
  PLURAL NOUN

- Everyone is in a/an _____ mood. And why not? There are
  ADJECTIVE

  cases of _____ to drink and _____ dogs to eat!
  PLURAL NOUN   ADJECTIVE

  Plus, it's a paid day off from your _____ job.
  ADJECTIVE

- The weather is always _____, so there are plenty of
  ADJECTIVE

  opportunities to _____ outside. Start an impromptu
  VERB

  game of _____-ball and light up some _____
  NOUN   NOUN

  -works . . . but be careful not to burn your _____ off!
  PART OF THE BODY (PLURAL)

Adult
MAD LIBS
THE WET WEDDING
The world's greatest *drinking* game

MAD LIBS® is fun to play with friends, but you can also play it by yourself! To begin with, DO NOT look at the story on the page below. Fill in the blanks on this page with the words called for. Then, using the words you have selected, fill in the blank spaces in the story. Now you've created your own hilarious MAD LIBS® game!

NOUN _____

VERB ENDING IN "ING" _____

ADJECTIVE _____

COLOR _____

NOUN _____

PLURAL NOUN _____

ADJECTIVE _____

NOUN _____

ADJECTIVE _____

COLOR _____

ADJECTIVE _____

PLURAL NOUN _____

NUMBER _____

VERB _____

NOUN _____

VERB ENDING IN "ING" _____

PART OF THE BODY (PLURAL) _____

ADJECTIVE _____

ADJECTIVE _____

THE WET WEDDING

It's the _____ you've been waiting for your entire life—
　　　　　　NOUN

your _____ day! Standing at the altar, you scan the
　　　VERB ENDING IN "ING"

crowd. Everyone looks _____, sitting in _____
　　　　　　　　　　　　ADJECTIVE　　　　　　　　　　COLOR

folding chairs on a beautiful _____ course. To your left
　　　　　　　　　　　　　　　NOUN

stand your groomsmen, dressed in matching blue _____ .
　　　　　　　　　　　　　　　　　　　　　　　PLURAL NOUN

The music begins to play and it's time for your _____
　　　　　　　　　　　　　　　　　　　　　　ADJECTIVE

bride to make her entrance. After the bridesmaids walk down

the _____ , you finally see her dressed in her _____
　　NOUN　　　　　　　　　　　　　　　　　　　　　ADJECTIVE

_____ dress. Hubba hubba—she looks _____ !
COLOR　　　　　　　　　　　　　　　　　　　　ADJECTIVE

The minister is about to begin the ceremony when you hear the

sound of _____ in the distance. Uh-oh! Only _____
　　　　PLURAL NOUN　　　　　　　　　　　　　　　NUMBER

seconds later rain starts to pour and all the guests _____
　　　　　　　　　　　　　　　　　　　　　　　　　VERB

in a panic. You and your bride manage to make it under a/an

_____ . She's _____ her _____ out
NOUN　　　　　VERB ENDING IN "ING"　　　PART OF THE BODY (PLURAL)

uncontrollably. "Look on the _____ side," you say. "Isn't rain
　　　　　　　　　　　　　ADJECTIVE

on your wedding day supposed to mean _____ luck?"
　　　　　　　　　　　　　　　　　　ADJECTIVE

Adult MAD LIBS

THE BEST BEER CHOICE

The world's greatest *drinking* game

MAD LIBS® is fun to play with friends, but you can also play it by yourself! To begin with, DO NOT look at the story on the page below. Fill in the blanks on this page with the words called for. Then, using the words you have selected, fill in the blank spaces in the story. Now you've created your own hilarious MAD LIBS® game!

TYPE OF LIQUID _____

ADJECTIVE _____

NUMBER _____

ADJECTIVE _____

NOUN _____

ADJECTIVE _____

ADJECTIVE _____

TYPE OF FOOD _____

ADJECTIVE _____

ADJECTIVE _____

PART OF THE BODY _____

NOUN _____

ADJECTIVE _____

VERB _____

PLURAL NOUN _____

A PLACE _____

NOUN _____

VERB _____

When you show up for a rooftop party, the _____ you
                                          TYPE OF LIQUID

choose to drink is very important. After all, the weather is usually

_____ , the party lasts for _____ hours, and you
ADJECTIVE   NUMBER

don't want to get _____ too early. So what should you drink?
                   ADJECTIVE

You take a look in the cooler, and the first _____ you come
                                             NOUN

across is a stout. You usually love to drink such a dark, _____
                                                          ADJECTIVE

beer, but it might be a little too _____ for this occasion.
                                   ADJECTIVE

You don't want to feel like you just ate a loaf of _____ .
                                                   TYPE OF FOOD

What about a wheat beer? It seems like the most _____
                                                ADJECTIVE

choice for a summer party. You love the _____ taste, but it
                                        ADJECTIVE

also gives you a raging _____-ache. In the end you choose
                        PART OF THE BODY

a/an _____ Light, your usual go-to. It's _____ ,
     NOUN   ADJECTIVE

easy to _____ , and goes with all the _____ you
        VERB   PLURAL NOUN

plan to eat. Only problem is you might have to make more trips to

(the) _____ than usual— _____ Light makes you
      A PLACE   NOUN

_____ all night long.
VERB

MAD LIBS® is fun to play with friends, but you can also play it by yourself! To begin with, DO NOT look at the story on the page below. Fill in the blanks on this page with the words called for. Then, using the words you have selected, fill in the blank spaces in the story. Now you've created your own hilarious MAD LIBS® game!

A PLACE _____

NOUN _____

PLURAL NOUN _____

TYPE OF LIQUID _____

NOUN _____

VERB ENDING IN "ING" _____

NOUN _____

PART OF THE BODY _____

NUMBER _____

ADJECTIVE _____

CELEBRITY _____

VERB _____

NUMBER _____

COLOR _____

NUMBER _____

TYPE OF FOOD _____

Adult MAD LIBS™
The world's greatest *drinking* game

THE VACATION CHECKLIST

You and your friends are going on vacation tomorrow to (the)

_____ and you haven't packed a/an _____ . Better make
_{A PLACE} NOUN

sure you have all your _____ covered and review your list:
PLURAL NOUN

1. Photo ID (your real one, not the one you use to buy

   _____)
   TYPE OF LIQUID

2. Boarding _____ for the airplane
   NOUN

3. Two _____ suits for the pool and beach
   VERB ENDING IN "ING"

4. Your i- _____ , for taking pictures and posting to
   NOUN

   _____ -book
   PART OF THE BODY

5. _____ pairs of socks and at least one nice pair of
   NUMBER

   underwear—in case you get _____ !
   ADJECTIVE

6. A hat, to protect you from the sun and make you look

   like _____
   CELEBRITY

7. An easy-to- _____ book for the beach like _____
   VERB NUMBER

   Shades of _____
   COLOR

8. SPF _____ . . . the last thing you want is to come back
   NUMBER

   looking like a/an _____ !
   TYPE OF FOOD

Adult MAD LIBS™

FAMILY VOLLEYBALL GAME

The world's greatest _drinking_ game

MAD LIBS® is fun to play with friends, but you can also play it by yourself! To begin with, DO NOT look at the story on the page below. Fill in the blanks on this page with the words called for. Then, using the words you have selected, fill in the blank spaces in the story. Now you've created your own hilarious MAD LIBS® game!

NUMBER _____

NOUN _____

VERB _____

ADJECTIVE _____

PERSON IN ROOM (MALE) _____

PART OF THE BODY _____

PART OF THE BODY (PLURAL) _____

VERB _____

NOUN _____

ADVERB _____

ADJECTIVE _____

NOUN _____

NOUN _____

PLURAL NOUN _____

VERB _____

PART OF THE BODY _____

PART OF THE BODY _____

NOUN _____

FAMILY VOLLEYBALL GAME

The world's greatest _drinking_ game

It's your family reunion, and you and _____ members of
                                            NUMBER

your _____ have gathered together to eat, _____ ,
           NOUN   VERB

and play a game of volleyball. But no surprise here—your

_____ uncle _____ is drunk off his _____ ,
      ADJECTIVE   PERSON IN ROOM (MALE)   PART OF THE BODY

and he's ruining the game. He already made your little cousin cry her

_____ out, and now he's trying to correct your form. You
PART OF THE BODY (PLURAL)

wish you could tell him to go _____ himself, but you can't
                                         VERB

because he's family. It's your turn to serve, and you accidentally hit

the _____ out-of-bounds. "Try it again!" your uncle shouts
         NOUN

_____ . You're feeling _____—why does he have to
   ADVERB   ADJECTIVE

be such a/an _____ ? You put the ball in play, and your uncle
                   NOUN

spikes the _____ back at you. You bump it to your cousin,
                NOUN

who sets it up for you. With all the _____ you can muster,
                                            PLURAL NOUN

you _____ the ball as hard as you can over the net, aiming for
        VERB

your uncle's _____ . The ball hits him in the _____
                PART OF THE BODY   PART OF THE BODY

and he falls backward. Maybe that will teach him not to be such

a/an _____ every time he comes to a family gathering!
        NOUN

MAD LIBS® is fun to play with friends, but you can also play it by yourself! To begin with, DO NOT look at the story on the page below. Fill in the blanks on this page with the words called for. Then, using the words you have selected, fill in the blank spaces in the story. Now you've created your own hilarious MAD LIBS® game!

NOUN _____

PLURAL NOUN _____

ANIMAL (PLURAL) _____

ADJECTIVE _____

ADVERB _____

NUMBER _____

VERB _____

PART OF THE BODY _____

ADJECTIVE _____

NUMBER _____

COLOR _____

PLURAL NOUN _____

EXCLAMATION _____

NOUN _____

ADJECTIVE _____

NUMBER _____

ADJECTIVE _____

It's game day, and I am standing outside the _____ -ball

NOUN

stadium. My buddy got us an extra pair of tickets to today's

game between the Cleveland _____ and the New York

PLURAL NOUN

_____, so I decided to scalp my tickets. Concessions these

ANIMAL (PLURAL)

days are _____, so I figure we can take the extra money to

ADJECTIVE

buy beers and hot dogs. "Two tickets," I say _____, so as

ADVERB

to not call too much attention to myself. But after _____

NUMBER

minutes, I still don't have any buyers. I start to _____ a little

VERB

bit louder, and out of the corner of my _____ I spot a/an

PART OF THE BODY

_____ woman walking toward me. "How much?" she asks.

ADJECTIVE

" _____ dollars." The woman reaches into her _____

NUMBER ... COLOR

purse and takes out a pen and pad of _____ and starts

PLURAL NOUN

to write something. _____—is it her _____

EXCLAMATION ... NOUN

number?! It isn't until she hands me the paper that I realize: This

_____ woman is actually a cop, and she's written me a ticket

ADJECTIVE

for _____ dollars! "Have a/an _____ day," she says.

NUMBER ... ADJECTIVE

MAD LIBS® is fun to play with friends, but you can also play it by yourself! To begin with, DO NOT look at the story on the page below. Fill in the blanks on this page with the words called for. Then, using the words you have selected, fill in the blank spaces in the story. Now you've created your own hilarious MAD LIBS® game!

EXCLAMATION _____

PERSON IN ROOM (FEMALE) _____

ADVERB _____

SILLY WORD _____

ADJECTIVE _____

PLURAL NOUN _____

ADJECTIVE _____

NOUN _____

ADJECTIVE _____

NOUN _____

ADJECTIVE _____

EXCLAMATION _____

PLURAL NOUN _____

VERB _____

ADJECTIVE _____

ADVERB _____

VERB _____

VERB _____

Adult MAD LIBS™

DRIVE-IN DISASTER

The world's greatest _drinking_ game

Me: _____ ! My date with _____ went
         EXCLAMATION   PERSON IN ROOM (FEMALE)

_____ wrong.
ADVERB

Friend: What the _____ did you do?
                     SILLY WORD

Me: I listened to your _____ advice on going to a drive-in
                           ADJECTIVE

movie. I did everything right. I picked her up on time and bought

all her favorite _____ , like _____ Patch Kids and
                 PLURAL NOUN   ADJECTIVE

_____ -covered raisins. Halfway through the _____
NOUN   NOUN

we started getting _____ and heavy in the backseat.
                   ADJECTIVE

Friend: _____ ! Then what?
            EXCLAMATION

Me: She asked me if I had any _____ for protection.
                                  PLURAL NOUN

Of course I did! So I put one on and we started to _____ . . .
                                                   VERB

but I got a bit too _____ . Let's just say it ended too
                    ADJECTIVE

_____ . You think she'll _____ me again?
ADVERB   VERB

Friend: Honestly, I wouldn't count on it. Maybe next time you

should _____ before your date!
       VERB

Adult MAD LIBS

ROCKIN' IN THE PARK

The world's greatest *drinking* game

MAD LIBS® is fun to play with friends, but you can also play it by yourself! To begin with, DO NOT look at the story on the page below. Fill in the blanks on this page with the words called for. Then, using the words you have selected, fill in the blank spaces in the story. Now you've created your own hilarious MAD LIBS® game!

ADJECTIVE _____

NOUN _____

ADJECTIVE _____

A PLACE _____

NUMBER _____

VERB (PAST TENSE) _____

NOUN _____

VERB ENDING IN "ING" _____

PERSON IN ROOM (MALE) _____

PART OF THE BODY _____

ADJECTIVE _____

VERB _____

ADJECTIVE _____

CELEBRITY _____

PLURAL NOUN _____

ADJECTIVE _____

VERB ENDING IN "ING" _____

PERSON IN ROOM (MALE) _____

Adult MAD LIBS™ — ROCKIN' IN THE PARK

The world's greatest *drinking* game

To: _____ .Bob@mail.com
ADJECTIVE

From: Music _____ @mail.com
NOUN

How's it going, buddy? I'm so sorry you couldn't make it last night.

The concert was _____ ! We were in (the) _____
ADJECTIVE   A PLACE

surrounded by _____ people and we _____ our
NUMBER   VERB (PAST TENSE)

way up to the front row, right up against the _____ .
NOUN

The _____ act was okay, but when _____ and
VERB ENDING IN "ING"   PERSON IN ROOM (MALE)

the _____ Burners took the stage? The entire lawn went
PART OF THE BODY

absolutely _____ . They played all of your favorite songs,
ADJECTIVE

like " _____ Me (Tonight)" and "The _____ Life
VERB   ADJECTIVE

of _____ ." At the end of the set, the drummer threw his
CELEBRITY

_____ into the crowd, and would you believe I actually
PLURAL NOUN

caught them? Talk about a/an _____ night! Sucks that you
ADJECTIVE

missed it. Hope you had fun _____ with your mom!
VERB ENDING IN "ING"

_____
PERSON IN ROOM (MALE)

Adult MAD LIBS

STUCK IN NEUTRAL

The world's greatest *drinking* game

MAD LIBS® is fun to play with friends, but you can also play it by yourself! To begin with, DO NOT look at the story on the page below. Fill in the blanks on this page with the words called for. Then, using the words you have selected, fill in the blank spaces in the story. Now you've created your own hilarious MAD LIBS® game!

ADJECTIVE _____

NUMBER _____

PLURAL NOUN _____

VERB _____

PLURAL NOUN _____

ADJECTIVE _____

ANIMAL _____

PERSON IN ROOM (FEMALE) _____

VERB ENDING IN "ING" _____

NOUN _____

PERSON IN ROOM (MALE) _____

PART OF THE BODY _____

VERB ENDING IN "ING" _____

TYPE OF LIQUID _____

NUMBER _____

ADJECTIVE _____

NOUN _____

There's nothing like a/an _____ traffic jam, especially when
ADJECTIVE

you're stuck in your tiny car with _____ friends and the air
NUMBER

conditioner is broken. You roll the _____ down and decide
PLURAL NOUN

to play a game of I Spy to _____ the time. Here are all the
VERB

_____ you spied:
PLURAL NOUN

- A license plate with a/an _____, hairy _____
  ADJECTIVE   ANIMAL

- Your copilot, _____, asleep and _____ on
  PERSON IN ROOM (FEMALE)   VERB ENDING IN "ING"
  her shirt

- An empty _____ of potato chips
  NOUN

- Your friend _____ drawing a picture of a/an
  PERSON IN ROOM (MALE)
  _____ on your copilot's face while she sleeps
  PART OF THE BODY

- A couple in the car next to you _____ loudly
  VERB ENDING IN "ING"

- A sign for the town of _____ in _____ miles
  TYPE OF LIQUID   NUMBER

- Two _____ tires
  ADJECTIVE

- Your "I heart _____" T-shirt in the rearview mirror
  NOUN

Adult MAD LIBS — THE ROAD TRIP

The world's greatest *drinking* game

MAD LIBS® is fun to play with friends, but you can also play it by yourself! To begin with, DO NOT look at the story on the page below. Fill in the blanks on this page with the words called for. Then, using the words you have selected, fill in the blank spaces in the story. Now you've created your own hilarious MAD LIBS® game!

PERSON IN ROOM _____

NUMBER _____

PERSON IN ROOM (MALE) _____

PERSON IN ROOM (FEMALE) _____

COLOR _____

PART OF THE BODY _____

COLOR _____

VERB _____

TYPE OF LIQUID _____

ADJECTIVE _____

A PLACE _____

SAME PLACE _____

PERSON IN ROOM (MALE) _____

ADJECTIVE _____

VERB (PAST TENSE) _____

NOUN _____

PERSON IN ROOM (FEMALE) _____

CELEBRITY _____

ADJECTIVE _____

Dear _____,

_{PERSON IN ROOM}

What a trip! I just came back from a/an _____ -week

_{NUMBER}

trip across the country with my two friends _____ and

_{PERSON IN ROOM (MALE)}

_____ . First, we went to Washington, DC, to see the

_{PERSON IN ROOM (FEMALE)}

_____ House and the Lincoln Memorial. Then we went to

_{COLOR}

Mount Rushmore, just to take a photo next to President Roosevelt's

_____ ! After that, we visited _____ -stone National

_{PART OF THE BODY}   _{COLOR}

Park. The best part? Seeing the geyser, Old Faithful, _____

_{VERB}

_____ out of the ground! Then we decided we were tired of

_{TYPE OF LIQUID}

all this _____ culture, and went to Las Vegas! Needless to

_{ADJECTIVE}

say, what happens in (the) _____ should definitely stay in

_{A PLACE}

(the) _____ . _____ got completely _____

_{SAME PLACE}   _{PERSON IN ROOM (MALE)}   _{ADJECTIVE}

and _____ all over the blackjack _____ , and

_{VERB (PAST TENSE)}   _{NOUN}

_____ went back to _____ 's hotel room. If anyone

_{PERSON IN ROOM (FEMALE)}   _{CELEBRITY}

asks, we never visited Vegas at all—we just got lost for days in that

_____ national park!

_{ADJECTIVE}

MAD LIBS® is fun to play with friends, but you can also play it by yourself! To begin with, DO NOT look at the story on the page below. Fill in the blanks on this page with the words called for. Then, using the words you have selected, fill in the blank spaces in the story. Now you've created your own hilarious MAD LIBS® game!

NOUN _____

NOUN _____

PERSON IN ROOM (MALE) _____

PLURAL NOUN _____

TYPE OF LIQUID _____

SAME PERSON IN ROOM (MALE) _____

VERB ENDING IN "ING" _____

NUMBER _____

VERB ENDING IN "ING" _____

PLURAL NOUN _____

SAME PERSON IN ROOM (MALE) _____

VERB ENDING IN "ING" _____

PLURAL NOUN _____

NOUN _____

PART OF THE BODY _____

PLURAL NOUN _____

VERB ENDING IN "ING" _____

ADJECTIVE _____

"And no one ever found the _____ murderer . . . but
NOUN

sometimes, late at night, you can still hear him chopping a/an

_____," said _____ as he finished his ghost story.
NOUN   PERSON IN ROOM (MALE)

You and your friends are camping in the _____ , and the
PLURAL NOUN

theme of the night is ghost stories. After throwing _____ on
TYPE OF LIQUID

the fire, everyone crawls into their tents. "Beware of the ax murderer!"

you hear _____ say as you get into your sleeping bag.
SAME PERSON IN ROOM (MALE)

After tossing and _____ for _____ minutes, you
VERB ENDING IN "ING"   NUMBER

start to hear the sounds of _____ in the distance. You try to
VERB ENDING IN "ING"

ignore them, but the _____ keep getting louder and louder.
PLURAL NOUN

Finally you unzip your sleeping bag and go outside only to find

_____ standing there. "Wait, if you're here, where's that
SAME PERSON IN ROOM (MALE)

sound coming from?" you say. Suddenly, you hear a loud chop and

you and your friend start _____ like little _____ . But
VERB ENDING IN "ING"   PLURAL NOUN

then your _____-friend crawls out of the tent laughing her
NOUN

_____ off. "You guys are such _____!" she says as she
PART OF THE BODY   PLURAL NOUN

plays back the sounds of _____ on her _____ phone.
VERB ENDING IN "ING"   ADJECTIVE

Adult
MAD LIBS™

HOW TO COPE WITH THE END OF SUMMER

The world's greatest *drinking* game

MAD LIBS® is fun to play with friends, but you can also play it by yourself! To begin with, DO NOT look at the story on the page below. Fill in the blanks on this page with the words called for. Then, using the words you have selected, fill in the blank spaces in the story. Now you've created your own hilarious MAD LIBS® game!

VERB ENDING IN "ING" _____

ADJECTIVE _____

ADJECTIVE _____

ADJECTIVE _____

VERB ENDING IN "ING" _____

VERB _____

NUMBER _____

A PLACE _____

ADJECTIVE _____

PERSON IN ROOM _____

NOUN _____

ADJECTIVE _____

ADJECTIVE _____

VERB _____

VERB _____

PLURAL NOUN _____

ADJECTIVE _____

Is Labor Day weekend approaching? That's a sure sign that summer

is _____ to a close. Does the idea of a/an _____
  _{VERB ENDING IN "ING"}   ADJECTIVE

workweek, _____ weather, and a more _____ dress
              ADJECTIVE   ADJECTIVE

code get you down? Are you already _____ down the days
                                      VERB ENDING IN "ING"

until Columbus Day? Here's some advice on how to _____
                                                      VERB

with the arrival of fall:

- Take a last-minute vacation. Even if it's only a/an _____-day
                                                          NUMBER

  trip to (the) _____, you can still make the most out
                  A PLACE

  of what _____ time you have left.
            ADJECTIVE

- If you've been waiting to ask _____ out on a/an
                                  PERSON IN ROOM

  _____, now's the time to go for it. After all, if he/she
    NOUN

  says yes, you're sure to have a/an _____ fall!
                                        ADJECTIVE

- Don't let the _____ weather _____ your social
                  ADJECTIVE   VERB

  life. Even if you can't _____ on a beach, you can still go
                            VERB

  out with your _____. After all, bars are _____ all
                  PLURAL NOUN   ADJECTIVE

  year round!